海水為什麼是鹹的

Sharing the Planet | Non-Fiction Series

Copyright © 2022 by Level Learning, INC.and Washington Yu Ying PCS™
Original and Edited Text Copyright © 2022 by Washington Yu Ying PCS™

All rights reserved. No part of this book in whole or part may be reproduced without written permission from the publisher.

Published by Level Learning, INC.
Content Contributors:
Washington Yu Ying PCS™ - Qianyi (Shirley) Zhang, Pearl Zao He You
Level Learning - Jingyao Qi

Illustrations by: Josh Taira

Leveling classification based on Level Learning standard.
For full description, visit www.levellearning.com

ISBN 978-1-64040-069-6
Traditional Chinese Edition

About Level Learning:

Level Learning provides a literacy focused curriculum specifically designed for K-12 Chinese as a Second Language classrooms. Our program offers 20 levels of specific and detailed objectives, leveled texts and passages, mastery-based online assessment, and analytics to enable data-driven instruction. Level Learning reading curriculum for both literature and informational text emphasize grammar and comprehension skills to help teachers develop confident and independent Chinese language readers. The non-fiction series of books are specifically designed to support our informational text course based on multiple national standards. To learn more about our entire offering, visit www.levellearning.com.

About Washington Yu Ying PCS™:

Washington Yu Ying PCS is a Mandarin English dual language immersion International Baccalaureate (IB) World school. Yu Ying's mission is to inspire and prepare young people to create a better world by challenging them to reach their full potential in a nurturing Chinese/English educational environment. Yu Ying's comprehensive IB, dual immersion curriculum equips students with global competencies for success in the real world. As a leader in immersion education, Yu Ying is determined to advance Chinese language programs and global citizenry education by helping other schools create and strengthen their Chinese programs. For more information, email: products@washingtonyuying.org

為什麼海水是鹹的呢？下雨的時候，岩石和土壤裡會有一點點的鹽溶解出來。這些鹽會被大大小小的河流帶入海洋。

慢慢地，海水不斷蒸發，可是鹽還留在海水裡。就這樣，海水裡的鹽變得越來越多，海水就變鹹了。

海水裡的鹽度越高,浮力就越大。

世界上有個神奇的地方叫死海。不會游泳的人也可以躺在死海的水面上，不會沉下去！這是因為死海的鹽度很高，浮力也就非常大。

我們來做個實驗吧。把一杯海水放在太陽下曬乾。你會在杯子下面看到一層白白的鹽。

鹽有什麼用處呢？我們的生活離不開鹽。鹽可以讓飯菜變得更美味、可口，我們的身體也需要鹽才能變得健康。

鹽可以用來洗東西。鹽可以消毒、殺菌。還有人用鹽水刷牙、漱口。

冬天下雪的時候,人們會把鹽灑在路上,雪落到有鹽的地上會融化得更快。

你知道嗎？鹽還可以用來滅火呢！你還知道鹽有哪些用處呢？

Glossary

	Pinyin	English Definition
海水	hǎi shuǐ	seawater
鹹	xián	salty
岩石	yán shí	rock
土壤	tǔ rǎng	soil
鹽	yán	salt
溶解	róng jiě	to dissolve
河流	hé liú	river
海洋	hǎi yáng	ocean
蒸發	zhēng fā	to evaporate
留	liú	to leave
鹽度	yán dù	salinity
浮力	fú lì	bouyancy
神奇	shén qí	amazing
死海	sǐ hǎi	the Dead Sea
躺	tǎng	to lie down

	Pinyin	English Definition
沉	chén	to sink
實驗	shí yàn	experiment
曬	shài	to bask in / to shine on sunshine
乾	gān	dry
一層	yì céng	one layer
用處	yòng chu	usefulness
消毒	xiāo dú	to sanitize
殺菌	shā jūn	to sterlize
刷牙	shuā yá	to brush teeth
漱口	shù kǒu	to rinse mouth
灑	sǎ	to sprinkle
融化	róng huà	melt
滅火	miè huǒ	extinguish a fire

www.ingramcontent.com/pod-product-compliance
Lightning Source LLC
Chambersburg PA
CBHW041223070526
44584CB00001B/68